'STOP HITTING mum!'

Children talk about domestic violence

by
Audrey Mullender, Sheila Burton, Gill Hague, Umme Imam, Liz Kelly, Ellen Malos and Linda Regan

Based on research carried out by:
The Centre for the Study of Safety and Well-being, University of Warwick,
The Domestic Violence Research Group, University of Bristol,
The Centre for Applied Social and Community Studies, University of Durham, and
The Child and Woman Abuse Studies Centre, London Metropolitan University.

Edited by Adrienne Katz of Young Voice

Listening and responding to young people

Contents

Introduction

Nick Ross

Domestic violence is a relatively new crime. Of course the behaviour is as old as humanity itself, which is to say as old as inhumanity, but for generations a man could beat a woman with impunity. Indeed rape within marriage only became illegal in 1994[1]. As cohabiting became fashionable this licence to be violent in relationships was surreptitiously extended to attacks on almost any woman by her partner. The bruises were hidden, the subject was not discussed. If the woman complained the authorities tended to advise that she should go home and make it up. When cases did come to court it was acceptable for the defence to argue provocation.

Little thought was given to the effects on children.

Over the last thirty years the women's refuge movement has developed. It now provides sanctuary for over 50,000 women every year, most of them with children, and has helped bring about a fundamental change in attitudes and deployment of resources. The police have become much more sensitive to complaints from women and more persistent and effective in their investigations.

There is a new awareness and a new openness. Society has become intolerant of violence in relationships. There is no justification for fatalism or defeatism.

But there is a long way to go. In 1996, the last time a specific study was conducted on this subject by the Home Office[2], only 12% of women who said they had been attacked had officially reported the offence. Even if reporting rates have doubled since then at least three-quarters of all victims suffer in silence.

This book shows eloquently how the children suffer too. Or rather, even better, it lets the children describe their feelings for themselves. This is a touching, very readable account of fear and pain, stoicism and bewilderment, desperation and hope. Out of the mouths of children comes a troubling indictment of the grown-up tendency to look the other way and not become involved. The more we listen to these children the more we understand that domestic violence is not a private matter but a profound moral and social issue. What goes on behind closed doors cries out for our attention.

[1] The Criminal Justice and Public Order Act (1994). The UK is one of only 20 countries where rape within marriage is illegal.
[2] Home Office Research Study No. 191 (1996).

Chapter 1 Living with fear
What did you see and hear?

Peta (9):

I've only really heard it, but I've never really seen it… I was thinking that my dad was hurting my mum. I could hear the conversations they were having and mum was saying, 'Stop it!' but, every time, I was crying and I didn't really want to listen, so I had to put my hands on my ears because I didn't want to listen. It was quite hard to go back to sleep because, mostly, I've been in my bed, most of the times… It's usually woken me up.

Salman (9):

He was grabbing her by the hair and trying to push her down the stairs… I was scared.

Naresh (10):

I saw my dad fighting with mum. I saw them arguing, shouting at each other and hitting each other. My dad used to do the hitting.

Natalie (12):

I was up in the bathroom running a bath. And then I heard this massive wallop. Mum had been hit from here (demonstrating) all the way over here (demonstrating) – right over to the fireplace. I came running down. mum was lying on the floor. I got ice and put it on her eye… I was very frightened. He went upstairs and mum had to go to hospital. I was very frightened. And the next day we left.

Eleni (17):

He had violent behaviour, everything. He was throwing the pushchair around; all these objects were just flying around the house.

Dawn (13):

There used to be bloodstains on the wall, but we've painted over it now.

What did you think was happening?

Kismat (12):

There was lots of arguing between my parents but I didn't understand why this was happening.

Ali (13):

I wasn't really sure what was happening at the time. I didn't really understand what was going on, but I know my mum and dad were fighting every day. I understand more now.

Dawn (13):

At first, I thought it was just verbal abuse, just saying things — I didn't think. Now he's just got more vicious. I think it's really life-threatening now, that he's really serious and means to do real harm to us, I just thought before that he was just — really he hated my mum, they didn't get along. But now it's just so much worse.

Lisa (15):

I don't know, really. It just kind of crept up on me. All I know is, one day I did know, so it probably happened bit by bit from me not knowing to me knowing. Then I could remember back to when things happened when I was younger, but I didn't think anything of it — like when my mum had bandages and she said she banged herself. But now I realize my dad must have done it, but they hid it from me and I just accepted it at the time. We even made jokes about it — like how clumsy she had been to bash herself, and things like that. Both my mum and dad, and me, we'd all make those jokes.

Knowing more than parents think…

Natalie (12):

That was the only time I saw it. It was behind closed doors. But I used to know and I would see the bruises that she had before that.

Ali (13):

When we were young, they tried to keep it away from us and argued in a separate room, not in front of us… As the fighting and arguing got worse, we could hear them arguing even when they were in a separate room.

Lisa (15):

So I just stay really quiet (in bed), so they don't know, and listen and check.

Heather (10):

They used to pretend it wasn't happening. But we knew.

Melanie (12):

Oh, I always did know, but… I don't say it to her (mother).

I see it all

Is there an incident you particularly remember?

Susanna (12):

He was just hitting her with his hands and shouting and swearing at her – saying that she's horrible, she's wicked and that she's not a very good mummy. Just saying all horrible things to her and really hurting her, making her cry, and mum couldn't do anything. I just called the police.

Kosta (15):

I remember him throwing the chair at her… a couple of days before we moved.

Dawn (13):

My mum used to cry a lot. She tried to commit suicide once with pills. We thought she was drunk because she was falling around and acting really strange. We then thought something was definitely going on.

Shamsun (10):

…it was my birthday… he threw the table and bashed her head on the unit.

Tasha (12):

When he punched her and hurt her jaw – that's when we went down the police station.

Salim (9):

My dad came up and (was) smacking my mum, and there was blood all over the stairs, and my mum rushed off and called the police, and everyone was talking about it … I was 6.

Underestimating the effects…

Louisa (13, has Down's Syndrome):

I was scared in case somebody came and got me… I woke up… and I was sick… I was feeling it on the pillow… The door was open and I stayed (sitting) up in bed… Then I put the light on and saw him kicking mum's head. My sister phoned the police and then I was crying and I wet myself. Then I went down the police station. Arrested him. And then he escaped and there was whole big police, guns and dogs look for my dad. Then I did a big diarrhoea. I sicked up a lot too. Then we had to go outside and that's it… I get nightmares about that.

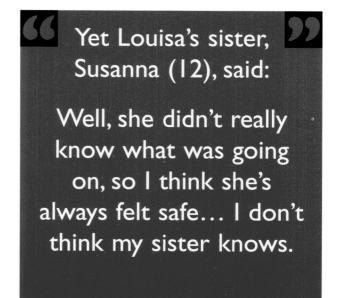

> Yet Louisa's sister, Susanna (12), said:
>
> Well, she didn't really know what was going on, so I think she's always felt safe… I don't think my sister knows.

Verbal abuse…

Dawn (13):

…he would say really ugly things about her – that she was worthless, stuff like that.

Yasmin (16):

He also called my mum names. He wrote on the streets that my mum was sleeping with her brother. My mum had to pay someone to get it cleaned off the walls. It was so shameful.

Threats and intimidation...

Mona (8):

He used to say, 'I am going to kill you at night-time when you are all asleep'. He used to come with an axe and say, 'I am going to kill you'. I used to get very frightened. We had a lock on the bedroom doors in case he did what he said. He once made a hole with an axe in my sister's bedroom door. Then he used to look through the hole.

Yasmin (16):

It was the worst part of my life – constantly being shouted at, frightened, living in fear. You will never know what it is like, thinking that every day could be your last day.

Kosta (15):

I used to – whenever he walked in the room, I used to feel that, if I said anything and he didn't agree to it, then – you know... Yiannis used to have nightmares. He never used to say what they were about, but they were only when he was around, not since then... my mum... virtually didn't want to leave the house alone.

Jealousy

Shazad (14):

Dad was very obsessive – if mum was talking to another man, dad would fly off the handle.

Ali (13):

It was over little things such as, if my mum talked to other men, my dad would get jealous.

Mona (8):

My mum wasn't even allowed to hang washed clothes outside because he would say she was going out so that she could look at other men. She wasn't allowed out in the front room because he would say she was again looking for men in the front street. I used to see all of these things happening in the house.

Susanna (12):

I think it's because he wants attention all the time. Wants everybody to love him and, if they don't, he gets mad.

Financial abuse

Naresh (10):

He also stole some of our money. It was about £80.

Mona (8):

I had £400 in my bank – he used to threaten me that he was going to get the money. My mum had savings for my brother, too, in the bank. Dad used to threaten my brother, too. He took my sister's savings and wasted it all.

" **Yasmin (16):**

He always made mum pay for everything. All that he had – house, taxi – my grandparents helped him to get … he was threatening me… I signed the money away… If I hadn't given him the money he would have killed one of us… He did have an axe. We were so scared. I signed only because I thought, if I didn't, he would surely kill me. "

Did you or your brothers or sisters get hurt?

David (12):

He was lashing out at everyone for no reason. He's hit me before... He was using his fists on me.

Joy (8):

My dad's really hurt my brothers and sisters. They used to cry.

Kosta (15):

I have seen him hit all the members of the family at least once... I remember my sister once... I remember him slapping her round the face... she was only around ten then. She didn't cry but she walked off and it kind of made her happy that he was going.

Mona (8):

He threw hot coffee on my sister, he used to bang her head on the floor and on the wall.

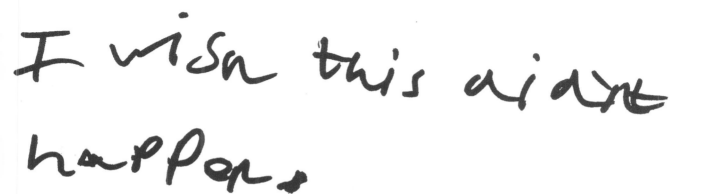

I wish this didn't happen

13

How did it make you feel?

Peta (9):

Really sad.

Natalie (12):

I was frightened and upset. I used to cry and cry.

Lisa (15):

It's like a nightmare and it goes on and on.

Shamsun (10):

The feeling that someone might know and they might tell my friends.

Louisa (13):

Upset. Upset and angry.

Sharon (15):

I used to feel I was bleeding inside.

Aziza (12):

I was very frightened. I thought I might get hit too.

Errol (8):

You know how it made me feel? It affected me a lot. It gets me all muddled and weird. I feel like it's all pressing outwards inside my head. Pressing outwards like this (demonstrates with his hands something bursting out of his head). I think it has frozen me up a bit inside.

Did it have any other effect on you or your brothers or sisters?

Dawn (13):

I used to have these pains – people said they were stress, or something. I stopped breathing… I used to get really upset and cry a lot.

Shamsun (10):

I couldn't really get to sleep.

Tasha (12):

It wasn't safe to go asleep in case he hit her… and I was always yawning and the teachers were telling me off for not paying attention… I had headaches all the time. At school the teachers just thought I was complaining all the time, but I wasn't. I really did have the headaches.

Sopna (9):

I used to wet the bed… I think this was to do with their fighting.

Salim (9):

When I was 8, I started kicking in my sleep.

Eleni (17):

Yiannis… will take his temper out – kick the wall or something if he doesn't have what he wants… If someone annoys me now, I just shout at them… Stelios is still quiet and he has to stay near Kosta. He won't leave Kosta. If Kosta goes out, he'll sit in here and wait until he comes back. He has to be near him.

Kosta (15):

He's like a shadow. If I was to stay downstairs for a few extra minutes, he would have to be down there.

Yasmin (16):

I've really missed out on my childhood. People say that it is the most carefree part of your life. This was not true for me. This was the worse part of my life – constantly… living in fear.

Chapter 4 Coping

Ways that children coped

From a group interview
(8 to 13-year olds):

We all cope in all sorts of ways... but lots of children are good at it. Children don't necessarily get upset and in a state about it. They can do fine with it. Some do get upset and they need support and caring because it is such a big thing. It is definitely really
a big thing for children.

Heather (10):

I used to put my head in my bedclothes and cry and cry… We (Heather and her younger brother, Ricky) used to hug each other… when they were arguing.

Shazia (8):

I wanted to hide behind the curtains, didn't want to see or hear it.

Shazad (14):

We knew inside about what was happening but we didn't want to talk about it – started doing other things… We would shut ourselves in one room and try to play with each other and shut the noise out.

Suresh (14):

I don't like to think or feel anything… I don't think about it. I don't talk to my mum or brother about it.

Ali (13):

I tried playing with toys or watching TV when all this was going on.

Mona (8):

When all this was happening, I used to be quiet. I used to pretend I was not listening. I used to watch TV or try to do my homework.

Someone to talk to

Lisa, (15):

It's good to talk about it… It's better like that.

Gemma (14):

I've always talked to my mum.

Kosta (15):

… she (mum) used to talk to us a lot. Whenever there's anything. Normally, if I was thinking of a question, even though I didn't want to ask it, she'd, like, explain what was happening anyway. She'd explain what was happening in the house and that was the reason why she was probably the closest person I spend my time with… and just being with Eleni – the fact that I could talk to her about anything.

Anjali (10):

Have someone to talk to you can trust – someone to help you understand how you are feeling… help you cope with the changes.

Peta (9):

They need someone to talk to. Because, if they were like me, sometimes… I'm really sad, I need someone to talk to. If they can't speak to their mum because, maybe their mums don't want to talk about it, then I think they need someone to talk to.

Dawn (13):

I said I wanted to talk about what was going on… she said, 'I don't think I can live with this man any more'. I was kind of encouraging her… because I knew what was going on then. I knew it was really serious. I told her that he was too dangerous because he used to beat her up.

> ## Johnnie (16):
> Talk to your parents more. I didn't and, when I finally did, it made me feel better... If you talk to your parents – sort it out in your mind – you'd feel a lot better... I think it makes sense to sort out exactly why and not let it hang around in your mind really.

But not everyone can...

Because I think it will hurt her

Peta (9):

I have said to her, 'Are you all right?', sort of, but I've never asked her what happened, sort of, how it happened. Just, 'Are you all right?' and stuff like that... She doesn't really talk to me about it (now)... I don't want her to think about what happened to her. If I know already, then I don't really want her to explain it because it might upset her about what's happened to her and may make her think about it. And I don't really want her to explain it to me... because I think it will hurt her. So I just leave it to herself.

Salim (9):

She gets upset if I ask her.

Some have no-one to talk to.

Shamsun (10):

Didn't have no one to talk about it.

Suresh (14):

No one explained anything at all.

Ali (13):

No one really talked to myself or my brother and sister.

Aziza (12):

Mum didn't explain to me where or why we were going. No one told me anything... I didn't ask any questions.

Shazia (8):

I am the youngest. They don't talk to me about what is happening.

Chapter 5 What children did

Did you try and do anything about it at the time?

Shamsun (10):

Cry and say stop it and he says, 'no I won't'. And I start to cry and (he takes) the mickey out of me by making funny noises and saying, 'Stop being a baby'.

Mostly shouting, screaming and crying...

Eleni (17):
Most of the time I used to scream at him to leave my mum alone.

Dawn (13):
When my dad started all of this, right, I would really get angry and start shouting at him, telling him off. I didn't hold anything back.

Shazia (8):
When I was little, I screamed and screamed and sreamed, 'Stop it, dad!'

Trying to protect mum...

Tasha (12):
I went in the room and I told him to get off my mum and he said, 'Go away, it's none of your business.' I said, 'Yeah it is, because it's my mum.' I took my mum out of the room and then he says, 'Mind your own business'. I said, 'No, this is my business.' I just took my mum out and she was trying to go back in there. I told her not to.

Errol (8):
I tried to help. I tried to guard my mum so he couldn't hurt her. I didn't talk about it with anyone. I used to run downstairs to see mum was OK.

Lisa (15):
... that's what I always do – I lie awake at night. I still do. I make myself be awake so that I can jump up when it happens and get between them... it's important that I don't go to sleep for my mum's sake... I have to help my mum... otherwise he might hurt her really badly.

Calling for help…

Eleni (17):

Half the time we had to call the police in. I think every house we moved to we had to call the police.

Susanna (12):

My mum had a phone in her bedroom. I just phoned the police… I did it loads of times.

Sometimes it got physical…

Josh (13):

Once or twice… last time I done it I had a knife in my hand and he tried to make me stab him with it, so I didn't bother trying to stop him no more.

Keeping themselves safe…

Salim (9):

… trying to find a big stick and just to keep it… We pushed this bed in front of the door.

Mona (8):

We had locks on the bedroom doors, in case he did what he said.

But not everyone felt they could do anything…

Gemma (14):

No, when he gets drunk like that, it goes on for hours. You just get out. You can't try and stop him – he's too big and fat to take on. I always stayed out of it.

Naresh (10):

I never tried to stop them. I felt I wanted to stop them but I didn't think I should interfere.

Ali (13):

No, I never tried to stop them because I was too young and couldn't really do anything to stop them.

Mona (8):

I didn't really try to stop the fight. I was too frightened. I used to think, 'He'll just beat me up, too', so I didn't interfere.

Peta (9):

If I was brave enough, I would have gone down and told him to stop, but I don't really think I am.

Chapter 6 Leaving home

Aziza (12):
If children need to leave home, they need someone to help them and they need somewhere to go.

When there is violence and no other solution…

Shazia (8):

Children need to move house – not to stay.

Yasmin (16):

She left him for us.

Sopna (9):

My mum left home first and went to the refuge. The police came later to the house and took dad away and collected our belongings. I was so scared and didn't know what was happening. I started to cry because I wanted my mum… I was only three years old at the time.

But a lot gets left behind…

Shazia (8):

Miss the other house and friends there – have to travel a long way to see them.

Shazad (14):

Leaving all our friends – I felt really sad. Had to miss a lot of school.

I miss my house. I like this home too.

Natalie (12):

I was pleased for my mum to get away from him. She was upset because of him. But I was very upset because I had to leave everything. Leave all my stuff. We just had the clothes we stood up in and we didn't come home for fifteen months. I had fourteen porcelain dolls and I had to leave it all behind. All my things. We just left… I was really upset because I had to leave Thumper behind… We had to leave him in the shed in the garden. I cried and cried. Because they don't have pets in the refuge. But then Margaret said he could come and live in the shed. We came with the police and got him. I used to sit down the shed with him and it was peaceful. A bit of peace. The children's worker always knew where to find me because I was in the shed with Thumper.

Peta (9):

… he made me leave my home. He made me leave all my best friends, made me leave all my things behind. Now I feel so sorry for my mum because she has to get all the money to buy all the new things for our new house – like beds and kitchen stuff and cookers – and they are so expensive. I feel like going there and taking all the stuff… he's got a house and he's got the money… But we haven't got anything.

Errol (8):

I have to get up very early and go by taxi to my school – it's so far from here. I still go to the same school. I'm good at school. And then I don't get back here in a taxi until late. I don't like it. My mum is better, but I'm not.

And sometimes it takes several moves to be safe…

Eleni (17):

We moved away from him and then, one day, his friend knocked on the door… and that's when we knew – that's when we decided it was better to leave… because he would find us.

Melanie (12):

We've been in three refuges. When I was in the second one, I liked it and, one day, when I was coming home from school, he knew what school I was at and I turned round and I saw him following me.

So even more gets left behind…

Eleni (17):

Annoying, actually, because at one point you make a friend… then, when we moved, it was a bit difficult because you either had to cycle or catch a bus.

Anjali (10):

… we moved to three different refuges… Annoyed, because I'd have to make new friends… because she said I'd have to change school and… I'd been there since nursery… We weren't allowed to take a lot of stuff with us because she said we'd be moving around a lot so we wouldn't be able to carry it a lot. Because I had like one big rucksack on my back and one big handbag. My brother had one big bag and my mum had… two black bags and a big bag… my brother brought like, a whole big plastic bag full of toys. I didn't get to bring none, just mostly clothes. I didn't get to bring a lot of things. Since that happened, I ain't seen none of (my friends) since.

What it's like in a refuge…

Peta (9):

… it's not your own home but, when you first come here you feel like it's going to be really weird, but I've been here five months now… once you settle in, it's like your own home but just with less things. You don't have as many things.

Natalie (12):

We helped each other… the other children helped. There were two children who helped me very much when I first went to the refuge. We help each other out. I've still got friends from the refuge. We stay in touch.

Not everyone has to leave for good…

Tasha (12):

We went to my mum's friend's house. But we only stayed there about two hours and then we came back because dad was gone. So we just came back and tidied up what he'd messed up, and went to bed.

The Children in my refuge

Chapter 7 Getting help
Who helped you?

Shazad (14):

Mum. Knew she would always be with us, keep us safe – everything will be OK.

Mum

Ali (13):

My mum has helped me the most… I can't really think of anyone else who has really helped me apart from my mum… mum has helped us the most at the time we left and she helps now.

Naresh (10):

My mum has helped the most. Other people around us have helped, too, but mum has helped the most all the time.

Sopna (8):

For me, being with my mum really helped – that was very important, that we were not separated from my mum.

Brothers and sisters

Shazia (8):

My brothers were very good to me when the fighting went on. They took me away and told me not to worry.

Dawn (13):

Sometimes I'd get really angry and I'd turn the volume of the music up really loud, and David would come and calm me down and, when he was feeling bad, I'd go up and calm him down. Sometimes, we'd just stick together – we'd talk together about what was going on, how we felt about it.

Heather (10):

… we used to talk together and sometimes we used to hug each other. And stay together when it was happening. I look after him.

Friends who could be trusted

Tasha (12):

Just being friends with people at school, because I only told one person – that was my friend. And she said her dad's done it to her mum, so we'd been in the same situation and we just talked about it.

Gemma (14):

I have really good friends at school. But they couldn't come round when he was here, he would be so violent to everyone. He drove everyone away. I'd be too embarrassed. It was too frightening for them but they come round now. Just this last few weeks – I had a sleepover last week. But we couldn't when he was here. Also, he's a racist and he's violent and two of my friends are black, so – But now they come round.

Peta (9):

… my best friend… I'd talked to her, but her family didn't really, they didn't really hurt each other – they used to argue, used to have the odd quarrel, but they didn't, like, hurt each other, so it was quite hard for to explain to her. But, my other two friends, I could just tell them… I couldn't keep it to myself… because I usually tell them everything. So I told them. They took it really calmly. They're not, like, 'Oh, we're going to tell everybody'. They were really, really good friends and, if you've got friends like that, I think it's really good to have friends like that. Now I haven't got them.

> ## Dawn (13):
> My best friend, B, she was having a similar problem. Her mum had run away from her dad's house because he used to beat her up… So we could share what was going on and try to keep each other going. We are really close friends because of that.

Salim (9):

I talked to my friend at school and said, 'If this happened to you what would you do? He said, 'I would go and help my mum and call the police'.

Peta (9):

… in this school, now, there used to be a girl who used to go to my old school. At nursery, we used to know each other from nursery… She's the only person I've told where I am. She really understands… She's the only one I can talk to about it, and she's really calm and she doesn't tell anybody.

Melanie (12):

I told my best friend only a little bit of it, because I don't really like telling people about it… I like getting it out in the open but it's just – it's my business, not theirs, and, just in case I had an argument with them. Supposing they – I doubt they would, but in case they let it slip out about it.

Other family members

Heather (10):

When we were (staying) at my auntie's, then we all used to talk about it.

Dawn (13):

My mum's sister is really strong… she really pushed my mum. Sometimes my mum would say, 'I don't know if I'm doing the right thing, really.' Me and my auntie would be like, 'No, not now that you've got this far'. She encouraged us a lot. Up to then, we thought there was no one to help us. Then she got my mum to talk to my mum's other sister, my mum's brothers – so, then, they started to know what was going on and now the family have supported us.

Eleni (17):

I wouldn't have minded going to live with my granddad… I used to escape there. We used to go there every summer.

Yasmin (16):

I used to sneak away from school to see my grandmother… Cousins, really nice. S was the closest. She told me to talk to the teachers and they would help. She would take me to the library and talk to me about how I was feeling.

Naresh (10):

Yes, my uncle helped my mum a lot. He helped my mum by giving his savings and money. He also bought me books and games for my brother. He was very helpful. He used to take us to fun places such as the fair. He used to go out with us when mum was not working. He helped mum – he made her independent. He gave her money and bought food for all of us. This uncle has helped us the most.

Other adults – friends, neighbours, at church

Aziza (12):

My mum's friend has helped the most by helping my mum… moving mum in her car to the refuge.

Peta (9):

There was a friend that talked to her. She helped her get some more clothes… This lady, she watched my dad while I stayed in her back garden with my mum. She watched my dad go out the door and get in his car and go away so (mum) could go upstairs and get some more things. So we went. I think that was nice because she was actually in her garden, sun-bathing. But then she sort of knew what happened because she's helped us before, all the time.

Naresh (10):

My mum found a friend… Ellie was a good friend to my mum.

Mona (8):

The Arab people who lived in the upstairs flat tried to help. They used to take us into their house, sometimes. They used to phone the police for mum.

Eleni (17):

I told someone in church but they were on his side anyway. That wasn't much help.

What about professionals, did they help?

Refuge workers (especially childworkers)

Natalie (12):

The childcare worker – she was great. If I was upset, she'd ask me why and she'd make it OK. She'd talk about it with me. The childworker was the best.

Sopna (9):

People at the Asian women's refuge helped the most... They did this by making our life happier, by taking us out. They made us feel better by taking everything out of our minds as if it didn't really happen.

Susanna (12):

... when I was in the refuge you have to talk, you have to at least say something. And, sometimes, you didn't really – you just made up what you were saying – you didn't really mean it.

Shazad (14):

Second time in the refuge, the workers were not very helpful. First time, workers really helpful – very good with us, talked to us, spent time with us. Second lot not as good – asked about you, but you could tell they were not really bothered – busy with mum.

The police and the courts

Natalie (12):

I'm still scared that he'll come to the door and hit her. I know he won't now, because it has all settled down, but sometimes I worry and I'm frightened. My mum kept explaining to me that he couldn't. She had an inch, inch – what's that word? Yes... an injunction, so he couldn't come and get her.

Group interview:

Try the police if it gets really bad. Get a grown-up to phone them if you don't feel able to. But, remember, the police can be more trouble than they are worth. If you are going to call the police... good to have talked about it with your mum first.

Chas (13):

I called the police, but they only let him back out after.

Salim (9):

The police took a long time coming and we were getting worried.

Mona (8):

When the police used to come, they would talk to my mum. She would tell them everything was OK and that my dad was OK. So they just used to go away.

Researcher:	When the police came did they ever talk to any of the children?
Josh (13):	No.
Researcher:	And had you ever been the ones that had phoned the police?
Josh:	Yeah!
Researcher:	At the police station, what were you thinking?
Tasha (12):	That they'd put us in a home, or something.

Psychologist

Susanna (12):

I don't think many children like it when they have to talk about their problems… I just think that you shouldn't have to just come out with it. It's not exactly like you just sit there and just staring into space, saying, 'I had a bad day at school'… you should be able to just play, or do pictures, or even write a little book, saying everything, and give it in every single day, showing how you feel and they could put it somewhere safe so that nobody else can read it. That would be good. I just don't like saying it straight away… when you just have to go there and they talk to you for ages, and you have to keep on answering the questions. It just gets boring… I don't like telling absolute strangers. I have to get to know people before I can tell them, really.

Court welfare officers

Kosta (15):

… he took mum to court about wanting to see us, so she (court welfare officer) came to ask us about what it was like, and that… sometimes I didn't really like talking about it. To be honest, I used to not know what to say. I used to think I was saying the wrong thing… the worst thing I could think of was actually having to see him again. Most of the time, as soon as they came, the first thing I was thinking of was that I've got to make sure that I don't ever have to see him. That was the main thing I was thinking about, which sometimes affected what I was saying. I remember saying – sometimes not answering the question because I couldn't… I spent around 15 minutes thinking about the question, trying to remember what it was. I don't think most of them believed me. I thought that, after saying it once, that would be it. But it happened about six times. Each time, the main question was if I wanted to see him again… Maybe it's just because I'm a child and they probably think that my mum got me to say whatever… One of them asked if it was my own views or not.

Teachers and school

Peta (9):

And then, that day at school, my mum took me and we went to one of the refuges. And she told my teacher what happened. She only told her a little thing and the teacher got worried and we left.

Shazia (8):

Mum told the teachers at school about trouble at home, we were moving. They didn't really say or do anything to help. They could have asked if I was OK, if I wanted to talk about it.

Mona (8):

The teacher wouldn't have believed me anyway, even if I tried to tell her. The teacher didn't like me and, if I had told her, she would probably have said that I made it all up. The teacher was always nasty to me, so I wouldn't tell her.

Melanie (12):

Only my form teacher (knew)… she was always nice about it, and then the Deputy Head knew about it.

Yasmin (16):

When he was after me, the schoolteachers were also quite good… The teachers got me a social worker.

Susanna (12):

I'm not learning very much… Sometimes 'cause I daydream, and just thinking when my dad hit me, and I want to really cry but I don't want to tell anybody. So I try not to cry and then I just don't do my work.

Social workers…

Yasmin (16):

The social workers – they were always there. The teachers had contacted them after I had told them a bit what was happening… I thought the social workers would help me and my mum, and if he harmed me they would know what happened. I think they finally made my mum see how risky it was for all of us to be living with him. They threatened that we would be taken into care if she stayed on after he had hit me so badly.

Eleni (17):

We had this social worker come round and he goes, 'Tell me in your own words'… I used to tell him. He would ask questions, then he would change the subject.

Sopna (9):

Social workers helped mum. There were white workers and black workers. They talked to make things better for her.

Kismat (12):

… social workers. I can't remember what they did but know they were involved. They all talked to mum about it. Yes, it did help. We were able to get help and get out. People talked to us. They asked questions. I can't really remember what sort of things they said or asked… I can't think at the moment how they helped. Maybe it was by talking to mum and helping her to go to the refuge.

Counsellors…

Sharon (15):

I've had a counsellor… it helps… The counselling helped.

Melanie (12):

At this school, there's a counsellor there and I went to her once… I talked to her about everything. That made me feel better.

David (12):

(Talked about) things like what's going on with mum and dad.

Dawn (13):

I thought they would think I was mad. I thought, 'I'm not crazy. I know what I'm doing.' But then, later on, I felt that it was good, actually talking to someone. I got a lot off my chest. Originally, I thought… 'I can deal with this myself.' I talked to her about what was going on. It sort of made me feel better – every time I left, I felt good. She's a really good listener and she gives advice and she does help… we don't just talk about what was going on, we talk about everything… She was the one who got me this job to design this cover for them. She did a lot.

Peta (9):

… with a lady here – she's a worker, Mary, she goes with me on Tuesdays. She takes me to the library sometimes, and I have my own little folder, I have my own little pad. I've got a picture of me at first, and I've written her a letter – where I am, why I'm here – and then we just write about how I feel each day, and I have to do a diary with her each day when I don't see her… I do that with her. That helped me as well because, if I get – I've stopped having nightmares now. Because I used to have nightmares about my dad finding us. It was even hard for me to explain it to my mum. And stuff like that.

Groups for children who have lived with domestic violence…

Peta (9):

I go to, like, this special club now… There's all other kids who've been through the same thing. They are not all in the refuge… most of them are coming from home and we all do… drawings about… abuse and stuff like that. Our mums go in a group, and we go in a group, and it's really nice. Because, then, I can talk to them about what I do and, like, how it happened and that, because they can talk to me as well… We talk about abusing and we have a theme each week. Like, say we were happy, what we'd, like, draw if we were happy. When we're sad – like when it happens – and sometimes they do puppet shows to show us, like, how it happened, sort of thing. We give them a theme and they do it for us. I did a play yesterday with my friend about abusing. It was only a really quick one but we did, like, a play. And we do – they give us pieces of paper most of the time. Like, we fill them in and stuff… Every Wednesday.

Some want to move on…

Sharon (15):

I've talked about it a lot. Now I just want to get on with my life.

Melanie (12)

I had another appointment with her but I didn't go… I don't like talking about it.

Chapter 8 Issues of community and culture

Ali (13):

Dad's brothers lived in the area. I think they tried to stop the fighting but they couldn't really do anything.

Dad's family is expected to help, in South Asian communities, but they may not…

Aziza (12):

Dad's mum and sister just made problems for mum so they didn't help. Mum's family helped a little.

Shazad (14):

They could have supported us more and told mum, 'If you break up with him we will look after you'. But, this didn't happen.

Naresh (10):

My dad's family could have helped. My grandmother was kind. She never used to let my dad come into the house.

So sometimes mum's family steps in:

Yasmin (16):

My nani (my mum's mother) and nana (my mum's father) have helped my mum the most. Her parents and brothers have always been there for her and for us. They bought this house for us – paid the deposit.

Shazad (14):

One uncle on mum's side really helped and looked after us. They were there for her and for us. We would get love and attention – no violence.

Mona (8):

My uncles and grandmother (from mum's family) also used to help. My uncle used to say he would kill my dad for what he was doing. My Grandad who is dead now, probably helped the most.

Aziza (12):

My mum's brother brought us back from the refuge – he contacted mum through her friend. We came back and lived with my nani (mum's mother) for a little while and then went back to the white house. Dad then started fighting again. That is when we moved into this house. My nani and uncle from my mum's family told my uncle from dad's family to help us with housing and so we moved into this house. We have been living here two, three years. I live here with my mum and little brother.

Family pride and shame...

Shazia (8):
Mum told us not to tell anyone about this – it will spread all over everyone else and other kids will know.

Sopna (9):
No, we didn't talk to anyone else because, if we did, then those people would talk to someone else and everyone else would get to know about it. I think it is too private for anyone to know.

Yasmin (16):
He wanted to keep us under his control – that is why he terrorized us. Mum stayed so long because of us and because of izzat, you know, 'What will people say?' She hid it from her family – wouldn't tell them how bad things were for such a long time… Our family is really big. Wherever you go, people would say, 'She told the authorities', 'Her dad's in trouble', '… brought shame to the family'.

Respect for elders, despite everything...

Ali (13):
We go to his shop sometimes, go the movies. He is OK with us. Dad – I have to respect him. Not for the violence, because he is my dad. It is against my religion – I have to respect my parents. If I was gora (white), I don't think I would have.

Yasmin (16):

In our family, you have to respect elders. Everyone would think that I had brought shame on the family if I had told people about him… I could talk to the social worker (but) I couldn't tell her everything – at the end of the day he was still my father.

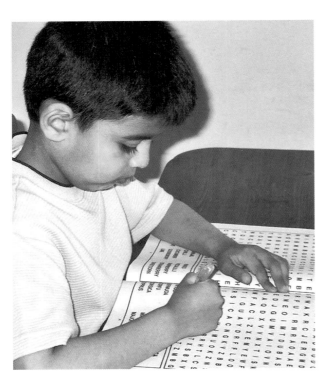

White people may not understand, or they may be racist...

Yasmin (16):

If you speak to adults, make sure they understand about your family and religion and they don't take things the wrong way. Like, sometimes, goray (white people) will not know about izzat and shame and they can make you do things which bring shame to the family. You are left without any help or support from the community, if they feel that you have gone against the religion. I don't say it is always right, but sometimes we have to sort things out in our own way – white people can never really do things in the same way if they don't understand.

Sopna (9):

Police... took us to the Asian women's refuge... Later, we did go to the (other) refuge... I didn't like it at all. Because we were black, the English people there were saying 'Look at those Pakis – they don't know how to do things'. They used to say a lot of nasty things to my mum.

Religious and cultural beliefs can help...

Shazad (14):

My religion kept me going. We believe that your time on earth is full of tests. Our life is full of tests. If you survive, your patience and strength will end your suffering. These are my tests. I had to stand by my mum because she was not in the wrong. That pulled us through and has made us stronger and better. We have been through a lot; we can feel for others and are better human beings.

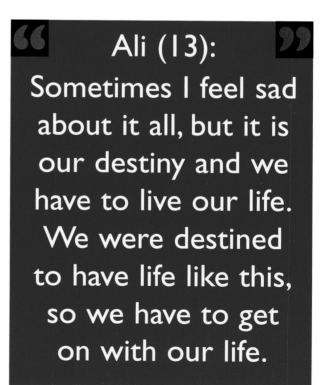

Ali (13):
Sometimes I feel sad about it all, but it is our destiny and we have to live our life. We were destined to have life like this, so we have to get on with our life.

stop fighting

Suresh (14):

It was my dad's fault. I know my dad created trouble. I still think it is my dad's fault.

Many were very clear about this…

Naresh (11):

My dad used to do the hitting… It was my dad's fault why the fighting took place… I still think he was wrong.

Salim (9):

My dad's fault.

Melanie (12):

My dad's… I hate him.

Sopna (9):

I know it was my dad's fault. I know my mum did not want to fight – she wanted peace and quiet. Yes, I still think it was my dad's fault. My mum's life has been made a misery and destroyed, and so were ours.

Though, when you're young, it can be hard to know for sure…

Errol (8):

I don't know whose fault it was. It wasn't my mum's fault.

Kismat (12):

I was very young when this all used to happen. I think it was my dad's fault… I felt then it was my dad's fault but now I feel sure it was my dad's fault.

Mona (8):

We all thought he was mental and that was the reason why he was behaving like that. He did go to the doctor, but the doctor said there is nothing wrong with him.

Dawn (13):

I just thought my mum and dad didn't love each other any more. I knew my mum wasn't doing anything wrong. I had no idea it was going to be this bad.

And you can have split loyalties…

Dawn (13):

Up until then… I sided with my dad most of the time because, right from when I was a little baby, I always wanted my dad. Until then, when I started realising, then I started to go with my mum, and then he started getting angry.

Susanna (12):

… my dad said it was my mum's (fault). I don't know why, but I believed him, and then I didn't know who to believe. If I believed my dad that it was my mum's fault, then my mum wouldn't love me. And if I believed my mum that it was my dad's fault, then my dad wouldn't love me. I didn't know who to choose. But I think it is my dad's fault really.

But, as you get older, you understand that the one who is aggressive and violent must take responsibility…

Melanie (12):

They have no right to hit women and they should know it hurts children a lot just to think about it. Some children might think it's their fault, and that, and they never get over it… They should just, if they want to hit someone, they should go into boxing.

Shazad (14):

He was unfair. The person who hits is in the wrong, they don't have the right to hit others.

Natalie (12):

I ask him sometimes, when I see him, why he hit mum. He always says that she hit him first and she started it, but she didn't. But I say to him that he was a boxer, so that makes it different.

Eleni (17) (Whose fault was it?):

Not my mum's because sometimes I'd go into the kitchen and he'll start on me for no specific reason.

Natalie (12):

It is the fault of the person who is violent, I think.

Sharon (15):

He controlled her. He thought it was OK to hit her and beat her all the time. He didn't think it was wrong.

Even then, you can be partly cross with your mum…

Sharon (15):

Oh well, all right. I thought it was both their faults because she was always depressed and tearful – but he was a bastard. He's mad. He's off his head. Really, you should meet him. I think he did too many drugs in the '70s!

Shazad (14):

It was dad's fault because he was violent. He should have talked it over instead of hitting, shouting… Like, if mum was in the wrong, you don't use violence. But I still think the same – her fault for going back to him. She was just doing it for us, but she should have finished it.

"I bash stuff every wer all!!"

Lisa (15):

Yes she often does (leave) but she always comes back within half an hour and she says that we are a family. But I think they should separate, but they won't. They need each other, I suppose, but they hate each other. My mum is scared of him, but she stands up to him.

Mona (8):

He used to chuck my mum out all the time but she used to go back to him so it was her fault for going back to him all the time.

Though a lot of mums do what they think is best for the children.

Shazad (14):

… going back to him. She was just doing it for us – she should have finished it… mum should have finished it then.

Yasmin (16):

She was really very sick. What could she do? She stuck with him because of us.

And, sometimes, you can blame yourself…

Kosta (15):

A couple of times I used to think it was my fault, because I used to be in the middle of it a few times; when the argument was going on or when, just before my mum divorced him, he was asking me to try and talk to my mum about it. Because I didn't really want to, I thought it was my fault that they fell out in the end.

Chapter 10 Afterwards

Has he changed?

Naresh (10):

I think he has changed and will change. I think he will become a good man.

Some men do...

Tasha (12):

He hasn't done it for a really long time now. I think I respect him now. I didn't use to respect him when he used to hit my mum, but I do now. He's sorted himself out and got a job and now I respect him.

But many don't...

Sopna (9):

Dad had come back and was living back home. It was going to be the same as before... we didn't want the same problems happening again, so it was better to leave home again.

Mona (8):

He would say everything will be OK and there would be no more problems. He would also say he would change, so mum had to return home. Nothing ever changed.

My house

Chapter 11 Do you see him now?

Salim (9):

I don't want to see him because he makes me upset.

Many children would prefer not to…

Peta (9):

No. What he did to my mum – I don't really want to see him. I don't forgive him… I don't really care if he's sad, because it's his own fault. He's upset my mum and he's done it quite a few times. We've given him chances but he's just blown it, totally, and we're never going to see him again.

Rizzy (11):

He comes here. We don't want to see him – shouts at us.

Ali (13):

I don't want to talk about this question.

Some do see their fathers but find it difficult…

Natalie (12):

Yes, I see him every week. It's all right now, but I get upset if he pumps me for information. At first, he used to come and stare in and I was very frightened. But I get on all right with him now. It worries me if he keeps on at me about mum.

Dawn (13):

Usually he starts off with, 'How are you? I love you. I'm your dad'… Usually when he calls, my mum's at work so I have to lie and tell him she's gone shopping. If he finds out that she's working, I'm not sure, but I know things would get worse. I don't know what we'd do

because he's not giving us money. But we just keep that secret for now. Then he starts – recently he starts asking if we're getting ready to go back to Africa because he thinks we're going back.

David (12):

… he's saying that I should go back home, back to Nigeria, all the time – that I should pack my bags and go back with him.

Some had contact for a time, but it had to be stopped because the violence continued…

Johnnie (16):

We used to. Up until around ten months ago. He started getting violent with me and my sister which he'd never done before… He started doing that and it was getting worrying because he was quite violent so we haven't really seen him since.

Melanie (12):

I used to visit a lot, but then my mum just ran into my dad, not long ago, and he hit her and that. He tried to smash a bottle round her face, or something. She wouldn't tell the police… I told her, 'Get the police.' Then she did because he – all the men were trying to hold him back and he was – he beat up quite a few men. Then my mum went to the police station and they asked her to do something. I'm not sure, but I think it was so that he could get arrested, but my mum didn't want to because she was too scared. I had a big row with her about it. We're OK now, though.

For others, it works OK, on the whole…

Rizzy (at 12):
Meet him – OK.

Mona (at 9):

He takes me and Rizzy out and, when we go to (the fair), he will go on rides with us… He is coming tomorrow and taking us. Sometimes we go to the town but I still think what he did was wrong.

Sharon (15):

I like to see him now we're away from him. Mum doesn't see him though. Thank goodness… He doesn't admit it (the abuse) or even think about it, I don't think. He thinks he's the king… I think he's an arsehole most of the time – excuse me – but I do kind of love him too, because he's my father. So I don't want to lose touch with him.

Susanna (12):

… my mum says we have to have it (contact) in a centre… my mum's scared, so we have to.

And some aren't sure how they feel about seeing their fathers

Dawn (13):

I wouldn't mind talking to him, right? But seeing him face to face – I'm not sure that I'm ready for that yet. I still have to get myself collected.

Melanie (12):

I think about going to see him but I'm not sure. I'm just scared because I remember he said to someone that he's going to get me, because he wants me to live with him.

Shazia (8):

She is never happy about us seeing dad.

Shazad (14):

I miss him… want to see more of him but my mum suffers, so it is up to her… He is really happy to see us – forgets what he did to mum… Sometimes she gets upset when she thinks about all that has happened.

Some, who are still scared, worry about bumping into their fathers

Melanie (12):

In case my dad just finds us. I'm always looking behind my shoulder... I'm having a nightmare every night about him.

Salim (9):

I saw him... when I was getting my hair cut. He was smoking. He saw me and I just turned my head the other way... My heart was beating fast.

Eleni (17):

There was one time on the train I thought I saw him. I was shaking so much... then, a couple of weeks later, my mum thought she saw someone exactly like him get off the same stop. Mum was so scared that she phoned the police to report that in case he might come.

Dawn (13):

I don't feel completely safe because my dad could turn up at any time.

But the courts often don't seem to understand these complicated feelings...

Timmy (8):	I don't want to go always, but I have to go because the law people said we had to.
Researcher:	Does your mum know you don't want to go?
Timmy:	Yes, and she's talking to the law people.

Chapter 12 What is life like now?

Dawn (13):

I don't feel completely
safe because my dad
could turn up at any
time.

Some are still scared…

Natalie (12):

I'm better than I was but I'm scared to go into the garden in the dark in case he jumps out.

Susanna (12):

I'm scared that somebody's going to come in in the night and try and do something to us… I have to sleep watching the two doors and with my back against the wall.

But most feel safe and much better away from the violence…

Kosta (15):

Once he'd left, then, to be honest, I didn't really need any help after that. Once he'd left. From the first day, I actually did feel a lot better.

Joy (8):

I'm happier.

> **Yasmin (16):**
> I feel really different. I can sleep without any fear. I can really live like any other young person in the community… Now he is not around to terrorize me I can get on with my studies.

Mona (8):

Some things have changed for us now. I get on better with my mum now. I can do a lot more things too… We get to see mum's family more now. My school is better now, too. I can concentrate more on work and don't have to worry about home all the time. I sleep well now I know no one is going to kill me while I am sleeping or burn the house down… I feel safe.

Sopna (9):

I feel safe now because I know no one can come and harm us now… I can really concentrate on things when I need to. I really enjoy school now – I don't like missing school at all. Before, everything was different. We all feel much better now… more friends and more people visiting us.

Sopna (at 11):

I feel much better about the violence. There are no more sad feelings about it. It doesn't upset me any more. Yes, I do feel differently about it.

David (12):

I feel a lot more calm and I haven't got that much headaches.

Naresh (at 11):

I feel different about the violence now. I like to forget it… it is in the past and I am not upset by it any more.

Johnnie (16):

Things couldn't be better. I'm not seeing all the things I used to see that I didn't want to. I hated seeing those things. And I'm seeing mum being happy instead, and laughing. Seeing mum smile every day. I get up every day, I have friends. I am happy, mum is happy.

Naresh (10):

We have more friends now. School is also good… I feel very comfortable and happy… I do sleep much better, I concentrate much more and I am very well.

Mums feel better, too…

Peta (9):

I think she feels she can do more things. She can do what she wants to do, really, because he didn't really let her wear certain things… I think she's free to do what she wants to do and I think she feels safer here. I think it's better because then she hasn't got to worry about my dad – what he's going to do next, sort of thing.

But they also still have things to sort out…

Ali (at 15):

My mother doesn't need him now. She is lonely, she should find someone else. I am not saying it is easy, but she is still young. She needs to get on with her life, just like we all will – all of us.

Shazad (at 16):

I feel that mum is quite lonely, managing everything on her own. Her family are all so far away – there is no one, really, who she can talk to or get help with.

Has anything good come out of it?

Shazad (14):

I had to stand by my mum because she was not in the wrong. That pulled us through and has made us stronger and better. We have been through a lot. We can feel for others and are better human beings.

Chapter 13 Advice to others

Aziza (12):

They need their mums to help them and talk to them. The children need their aunties. They need their friends when problems are in the house.

What do children need?

Kosta (15):

Just knowing that it's not going to happen again.

Susanna (12):

Someone to talk to… someone who they can really, really, really trust. Like, maybe one of their really good friends.

Dawn (13):

Some kind of support, because I know it was horrible because no one was there. They need to know that someone is backing them up.

Melanie (12):

A counsellor, or someone like that. Someone that would just take them out, and that, and that would make it easier for them. Make them feel good about themselves and make them feel it wasn't their fault.

Suresh (14):

… safe space and not to get involved in fights… love and care… support… good places to live and money to get there… counselling service.

Naresh (10):

If children need to get away, they need someone to talk to. They need to go far away to be safe. They need a safe place where they can be happy and get away from problems.

> **Mona (8):**
> Children need to take clothes with them if they leave home. They need friends and relatives to give them a good home, a nice clean home. The children need blankets, coats, and everything else you would have in a home.

Tasha (12):

Somewhere they can go, like when their parents are arguing, that they can get out of the house.

Salim (9):

Someone to tell dad to stop it. Take him away.

Shazad (14):

Someone to trust. A nice environment, homely, that will raise their confidence. Toys, games, to occupy their time. Someone to talk to about how they are feeling and help them to understand why it is better that they have left. Sometimes, when you are younger, you cannot understand why it is better to leave your home and family, to go and live somewhere else with other people you don't know. You need people to understand how you are feeling and help you to cope with the changes.

Yasmin (16):

Children should be able to have a life like a child, not live like criminals… It should be a carefree time – love and affection in the family.

Advice to other children

Yiannis (12):

Move somewhere where your dad don't know.

Suresh (14):

Talk to your parents and talk to someone else.

Shazad (14):

… talk about what's happening to parents or to mum. Don't keep it in… Try and persuade mum to get help, see someone. Try and get away before it is too late. Like the young woman (from the local community who) has just been stabbed to death by her husband. My mum would have been in that situation if she hadn't been strong enough to leave and get help from a friend… Try and help your mum be strong. Tell teachers so they can get help for your mum. Be there for your mum, talk to her about what's happening, keep your mum strong.

Sharon (15):

Get help…talk to people… don't carry it yourself. And get away from the violence. No one should have to live with violence, should they?

Kosta (15):

Well, if they have any brothers and sisters, the best thing, in my opinion, is to speak to them about it and, if they are older than you, then they can speak to their parents for you, so you don't directly have to do it yourself.

Shazia (8):

Tell the teacher or someone you trust and love about how you feel.

Salim (9):

… phone the police and try to stop them fighting. Tell whoever is doing it not to do it again and say sorry… Run out of the house.

Naresh (10):

Refuges are good. Children need someone to talk to.

Natalie (12):

… don't worry about it. It will soon pass. The childcare workers will help you. Don't worry. You will be safe in the refuge. Don't worry.

Peta (9):

… don't worry, I've been through the same thing. If you forget about your dad, all your worries will go away… Just think about your mum, really, care for your mum. And, if you've got brothers and sisters, make them feel better, and just forget about it, really.

Ali (13):

Ignore it – keep yourself busy. Go to a different room and put on headphones… keep yourself occupied. Don't give yourself time to think and get upset.

Kismat (12):

Don't take it all too seriously. Don't think that the world is going to end. Don't think of all the bad things all the time.

Dawn (13):

Sit down, think about what's going on. Try and keep a level head… I know I used to get really upset and cry a lot. Don't do that because it only makes you weaker. Just think about what's going on and try and compose yourself because, once you stop and think, your mind arranges itself and you know what to do.

Advice to parents

Sopna (9):

Tell them they should be looking after you instead of fighting with each other. Tell your parents that you should be the most important things to them in the world, rather than fighting… Why are you fighting? You can lose each other and you can lose your children. There is no good in fighting, so don't fight.

Kismat (12):

Try and explain to the children in a way they can understand.

Dawn (13):

Talk to your children. No one told me what was going on. I had to sort of piece it together myself. Talk to them, tell them what's going on. If something's going on, I think they have the right to know. Most people tend to think that children are too young to understand – they're not.

Yasmin (16):

If you want to argue, do it away from the kids – when they are at school, out of the house. You don't think about it – it hurts the children. They can't concentrate at home or in school. They are scared and frightened. It is not fair on them to put them through this.

Advice to mothers

Rizzy (12):
Tell us what is happening.

Shazad (14):
Think about your children – they are being affected by what they are living with. You are not helping them by staying, even if you think you are, because the fighting will go on. It will affect them and their moral confidence. They are suffering. Some can't take it and may become ill. It doesn't work out by staying.

Kosta (15):
In our case, I'd tell my mum that, in the circumstance at that time, if I was this age now, I would have told her straight away, from the the first thing that happened, to leave and never see him again.

Yasmin (16):
They need to get away – a long way from him, so that he can't find them. If it is that bad, mums should leave. They can go and live with their family, but these troubles won't stop – he will break down their door. They need to go away so that he can't find them… Leave. It is better for you and your kids. You have to choose between the kids and your husband if things are really bad. You chose to marry him but the kids did not choose you as parents. You have to think about them. The kids are suffering – you have to make a decision.

Mona (8):
Leave your husband and his home. Go somewhere better with the children.

Melanie (12):
They should try and just get out as soon as it happens and just, like, start a new life with their children, straight away.

Peta (9):
I would say to them, (children) hate it as much as you hated having it done to you. They hated it as much as you hated having it done. I suppose it's the same as them getting hurt because it's, really – I think they get more upset because, if they care about their mums and, say they are really attached to their mum, they didn't like their dad at all – their dad did that.

Natalie (12):
Don't go back to them. That's all really.

Advice to abusive fathers and step-fathers

Rizzy (12):
Stop shouting and hitting.

Shazia (8):
Children are frightened and unhappy. Stop hitting mum.

Tasha (12):
… try and keep your temper. You scare the mother and the children.

Josh (13):
Go somewhere else.

Peta (9):
I would say to him – well, I did say to him, the night that he took me back – I said, 'Why did you hurt mum?', and he was trying to get out of the conversation, like she was really naughty. And I'm, like, 'No'. Then, like, 'Yes, she is. Now let's talk about something else', sort of thing. But I went back and I

told him. I said, 'You wouldn't really like it if mum came up and was beating you up, sort of thing, and hurt you. Then you had to run away… You wouldn't like it if you were getting picked on… It's not fair, just because you think you're bigger. You're bullying mum. I think you should go back and say you're sorry. She doesn't ever want to see you again for what you did. So we don't like you any more. We don't want to live with you because you're horrible to her.' And he's ruined her life, really.

Shazad (14):

Children are suffering because of what you are doing to their mum. They are frightened and sad because they are different and not like other children who have happy homes. Violence is no way to solve problems – it doesn't work. Don't give this example to your children. They are frightened of you, even though they may love you.

Susanna (12):

… what you're doing is wrong and you shouldn't be doing it. If you're going through anything, whatever's making you mad, to lose your temper and take it out on your wife, you should go to somebody and talk to them about it because it will make things a lot better… And, if it doesn't work out, then maybe you should just leave the wife.

Advice to professionals

Tasha (12):

(Children) need support and, like, care. People will have to be friendly to them because they'd most probably be scared.

Sopna (9):

The children need someone to look after them. If their mum or dad are taken to prison or the police station to answer questions, children need someone to be with them. They should think about this.

Group interview:

Children may want someone to take responsibility for them, instead of them doing it… to take the weight off their shoulders.

Natalie (12):

Get more childworkers. There should be one for each refuge and… they need extra help in the holidays.

Eleni (17):

I think best, when they're young, to let them say their feelings. I had no one to talk to.

Don't underestimate young people, they can help make decisions…

Dawn (13):

Before she wanted to go for the divorce she was thinking about it. She said 'I don't think I can live with this man anymore' and I was kind of encouraging her, telling her that – because I knew what was going on – that I knew it was really serious. I told her that he was too dangerous.

Group interview:

Grown-ups think they should hide it and shouldn't tell us, but we want to know. We want to be involved and we want our mums to talk with us about what they are going to do – we could help make decisions.

Chapter 14 Looking to the future

Susanna (12):

I'm not getting married...
They might be like my dad
and then they'll hit me.
Then I'll have to go to
another refuge, and I
don't want that to
happen to my
children.

Views on marriage, relationships and having children...

Melanie (12):
I've gone a bit off men.

Gemma (14):
Well, I'm not going to get married. Never!

Yasmin (16):
All my experience, and mum's, has really made me think. I know that I want to get married to someone from home – apna (from my own community) not gora (white) – but not someone from Pakistan. There is a lot of difference. You grow up in two different worlds. It is always difficult for men to be dependent on the wife... I want to study and make something of my life. Marriage is not everything. I will marry when I think the time is right... I would want to be an equal partner. But if my husband acts funny, like dad, I will leave him... I will never put my children through this.

Shazad (14):
Mum has been brought up in England, got married to a Pakistani... I would never get married like that – arranged marriage because your parents say so. They were too different... Always see that you have something in common. It should be a partnership. You don't get married because your parents say so. They were so different, like a dog getting married to a cat – nothing in common.

Dawn (13):

I decided I don't want to get married. Definitely don't want to... Once you get married, there's that tension. You think, 'Oh, I'm stuck with this person for the rest of my life...' You feel you can't get away from them. I just feel that way.

Suresh (14):

I just don't accept violence between a man and a woman… it's not right hitting a woman, she cannot hit back in the same way. That is why men hit women – they know that they cannot hit back… I don't believe in violence… Once a man hits a woman, that relationship is broken and should never carry on. Got to respect women. Things are more equal now. Yes, better than before. Women are working, men are helping in the house – not always, but more now. It goes both ways – both must respect. The man must respect the woman. If the woman does not respect him… leave her, don't resort to violence.

Eleni (17):

I've always said that I'd never treat my children like he treated us.

Boys may fear growing up like their fathers…

Errol (8):

I'm frightened I'll be like it when I grow up… Sometimes I feel I might be really mean, like he is, when I grow up but I hope not to be. I've talked with my mum about it. I think it's really bad to be mean but I worry I might be. I might grow up to be mean and nasty like my dad. What do you think?

Shazad (14):

We want to learn from my parents' mistakes so that it doesn't happen to us… I will never be like him.

Josh (13):

Don't be like that when you're older.

Moving on with your life…

Ali (13):

Now, we just want to get on with our life. Now, I keep my mind on school, GCSEs. This helps to get on with life.

> ## Dawn (13):
> I want to take my exams, get a good job, live with maybe two dogs and a cat. Just want to enjoy my life.

Ali (at 15):

Being without him is good. We have taken his place – try to look after mum and my sister… I am going for work experience… I think that I have moved on. I am older now… We are grown up and we can take on some responsibilities.

Shazad (14):

I am the man in the house now. We have lived a hard life – we have become tough… We have made a new life for ourselves… It was a nightmare while it lasted… but you move on and put it behind you. Sometimes I talk to my brother about the future, about our lives.

Errol (8):

I… want to stay in the old house but get things to change. We could change it all round – change the furniture, and start again… We could change it around, to take out all the terrible memories for her. We've got all our friends there to help. We could get a guard dog. That's what I'd like to do… It's really hard on kids. I want to make an effort to help her. I'm going to do everything I can to be helpful. I want to help out with the washing up. Can I go now?

Yasmin (16):

I will stand by my mother – she needs me. Who does she really have, except us? But you know, through it all, I have survived. I am happy now, it all seems a bad dream… I will show him what I can make of my life, no thanks to him… If I get a job, I can stand on my own feet – share mum's responsibilities. It will also give me a chance to move on with my life. I need someone to tell me what's on offer, what choices I can make – the pros and cons – understanding my family background.

Who can I talk to?

If you, a member of your family or someone you know is experiencing domestic violence there are a range of organisations that can help.

IN THE EVENT OF AN EMERGENCY CALL 999

National Helplines

■ Childline freephone 24 hours for confidential advice and counselling.
0800 1111

■ The Samaritans offer advice and counselling and can put you in touch with a relevant organisation.
08457 90 90 90
www.samaritans.org.uk

■ Women's Aid 24 hour helpline offering help with finding somewhere safe for women and children to stay, counselling, legal advice and 'language line' providing you with translators.
England & Wales 08457 023 468
www.womensaid.org.uk
Northern Ireland 02890 331 818
www.niwaf.org
Scotland 0800 027 1234
www.scottishwomensaid.co.uk
Rep of Ireland 1800 341 900
www.womensaid.ie

■ National Child Protection Helpline (NSPCC) freephone 24 hours for counselling and practical advice for young people and adults.
England & Scotland 0808 800 5000
Wales 0808 100 2524
Rep of Ireland 1 800 666 666

■ Asian Helpline. Lines open Mon – Fri 11am – 7pm.
0800 096 7719
help@nspcc.org.uk

■ Refuge Crisis Line 24 hour national crisis line providing help with emergency accommodation needs.
08705 995 443

■ Get Connected. Helping you connect to the right organisation for advice and to find a safe place to stay. Language line available for those who may require a translator. Lines open every day 1pm – 11pm.
0808 808 4994

■ Broken Rainbow helpline for lesbians, gay men bisexuals and transgender people who are experiencing domestic violence. Lines open Mon – Fri 8am – 5pm.
07812 644 914

■ Free Message Call Home confidential, non-traceable service for those wishing to pass message on to people at home without communicating directly.
0500 700 740

Crime

■ Victim Support offers help whether the crime is recent or past providing information, practical help and support. Lines open Mon – Fri 9am – 9pm, Weekends 9am – 7pm, Bank Holidays 9am – 5pm.

UK 0845 30 30 900

Rep of Ireland (01) 8780 870

supportline@victimsupport.org.uk

■ Rape Crisis Federation Wales and England can put young girls and women in touch with their nearest rape crisis centre providing support, information, advice and counselling. Lines open Mon, Thurs and Fri 10am – 1pm and Tues 2pm – 7pm.

0115 941 0440

www.rapecrisis.co.uk

Ethnic/ Religious Groups

■ Jewish Women's Aid offers advice and support to Jewish women and girls who are experiencing domestic violence. Freephone Mon, Wed and Thurs 9.30am – 9.30pm.

0800 591 203

■ Southall Black Sisters provides both crisis intervention and longer-term casework for Black and Asian girls and women who are experiencing domestic violence and conflict in their family or community. Lines open Mon to Fri 10am – 4pm.

0208 571 9595

■ Muslim Women's Helpline provide counselling, advice and referrals to refuges for Muslim girls and women. Service available in Arabic, Urdu, Punjabi and English. Lines open Mon to Fri 10am – 4pm however they will return your call if you leave a message outside these hours.

0208 904 8193

Housing

■ Shelterline 24 hour helpline for the homeless or people with urgent housing concerns.

0808 800 4444

Rights and Legal Advice

■ The UN Convention on the Rights of the Child 1990 contains 54 articles setting the standards for the treatment of children.

Article 12 states:

1. States Parties shall assure to the child who is capable of forming his or her own view the right to express those views freely in all matters affecting the child, the views of the child being given due weight in accordance with the age and maturity of the child.

2. For this purpose the child shall in particular be provided the opportunity to be heard in any judicial and administrative proceedings affecting the child, either directly, or through a representative or an appropriate body, in a manner consistent with the procedural rules of national law.

■ The Children's Legal Centre free and confidential legal advice and information service for children, young people and those who have concerns about them.

01206 873820

www.childrenslegalcentre.com

■ Children's Law Centre free and confidential advice and information about the rights and laws that affect children and young people in Northern Ireland. Lines open Mon to Fri 9.30am – 4.30pm.

0808 800 5678

www.childrenslawcentre.org

■ Free Legal Advice Centres offer advice to people living in the Republic of Ireland.

Ireland 01 874 5690

www.flac.ie

Further Counselling/ Reassurance

■ www.there4me.com confidential online advice for teenagers where you can email a letter to an agony aunt or contact a there4me adviser in real time.

help@there4me.com

■ www.itsnotmyfault.org.uk online advice and support for children, young people and parents about family conflict.

■ Relate Line confidential counselling for children young people and adults. Lines open Mon to Fri 9.30am – 4.30pm.

0845 130 4010

■ Parentline Plus 24 hour helpline offering advice to parents on what can be done for them and their children.

0808 800 2222

Regional

■ SHE Helpline 24 hour helpline covering Essex, East London, Kent, Norfolk, Suffolk and Cambridgeshire offering referral to a refuge including Asian, Black and Irish refuges if requested, an on site solicitor, specialist children's counselling and a mental health surgery.

01702 300006

■ The Barika Project joint partnership between NCH and Tower Hamlets Women's Aid providing help to young women and their parents to get families back on track and to strengthen relationships. Includes individual, group, family sessions and outreach work. Agency and self-referral. Information pack available from NCH Children's Fund Project, Jack Dash House, 2 Lawn House Close, Marsh Wall, London, E14 9YQ.

■ Staying Put is a service for women experiencing domestic violence - who want the violence to stop but do not want to leave home. The violence may be from a partner, ex-partner or family member. It is for women and children who live in the Bradford district. 24 hour freephone helpline

0800 0856206

Useful Websites

■ www.bbc.co.uk/health/hh the BBC's 'Hitting Home' site provides advice and relevant links to organisations for children, young people and adults including information on the effects of domestic violence on children, pregnancy and domestic violence, children's legal rights and sources of support.

■ www.hiddenhurt.co.uk written by a survivor of domestic violence this website provides extensive advice and information on all areas of abuse for children, young people and adults with links to relevant organisations.

Acknowledgements

We would like to thank all the children and young people whose words and drawings appear in this book. Our thanks go to Hilary Saunders of Women's Aid, for advice and children's drawings.

Through Wendy Gledhill of Staying Put, we would like to thank Z who donated his drawings. Staying Put is a service for women experiencing domestic violence – who want the violence to stop but do not want to leave the home. It is for women and children who live in the Bradford District.

NCH – The Barika Project

Additional drawings were supplied by Linda St Louis, Project Co-ordinator of 'The Barika Project', a working partnership between NCH and Tower Hamlets Women's Aid. The project supports young women between the ages of 5 and 13 and their mothers who are living with domestic violence. Barika adopts a solution-focused approach in helping families to get their lives back on track after domestic violence'

Marie Hartley of Hyndburn and Ribble Valley Domestic Violence Forum supplied a drawing collected from Blackburn refuge.

Thank you to Lisa Brook for background research

All photographs are models, all children's names have been changed.

The research behind this book

We interviewed 54 children who had lived with domestic violence and we have put some of the main things they told us in this book. Other children, while living in refuges, or being helped by Staying Put in Bradford, contributed the drawings.

The research that enabled us to talk to the children was funded by the Economic and Social Research Council in its 'Children 5-16 Programme'. It was co-ordinated by the Centre for the Study of Safety and Well-being at the University of Warwick and was conducted by researchers from the Domestic Violence Research Group at the University of Bristol, the Community and Youth Work Studies Unit at the University of Durham and the Child and Woman Abuse Studies Unit at London Metropolitan University.

Other elements of the research were interviews with mothers and professionals, and a large survey of children in primary and secondary schools to find out what they knew and thought about domestic violence. The whole study is written up in the book Children's Perspectives on Domestic Violence, which was published in 2002 by Sage in London. The authors were Audrey Mullender, Gill Hague, Umme Imam, Liz Kelly, Ellen Malos and Linda Regan.

Another useful book, because it tells professionals how to provide the best services they can to support children and their families when domestic violence has taken place, is by Cathy Humphreys, Marianne Hester, Gill Hague, Audrey Mullender, Hilary Abrahams, and Pam Lowe. It is entitled From Good Intentions to Good Practice: Working with Families where there is Domestic Violence and was published in 2000 by the Policy Press in Bristol.

We would like to thank Adrienne Katz and Young Voice for the opportunity to give children a voice in this book. We would particularly like to thank the children themselves who talked to us so bravely and who had such important things to say.

The Authors, September 2003

Young Voice is a registered charity working to make young people's views and concerns heard. Our work is carried out in partnership with children and young people. They have equal status, with researchers in everything we do. Our protocols offer anonymity, dignity and respect, with equality for all.

Young Voice offers research, projects, publications, training and commissioned work.

Among our publications that might have a link to the issues in this book are:

'Bullying in Britain – Testimonies from Teenagers', in which violence is discussed.

'Parent Problems! Conversations with children when parents split up'.

'Fitting in or Fighting Back?' gangs, bullies, weapons, drugs and disruptive behaviour.

Further copies of this book and these titles are available from www.young-voice.org